SEAMUS HEANEY

District and Circle

faber and faber

First published in 2006
by Faber and Faber Limited
3 Queen Square London WC1N 3AU
Published in the United States by Faber and Faber Inc.
an affiliate of Farrar, Straus and Giroux LLC, New York

Photoset by RefineCatch Ltd, Bungay, Suffolk
Printed in England by T.J. International Ltd, Padstow, Cornwall

The right of Seamus Heaney to be identified as author
of this work has been asserted in accordance with Section 77
of the Copyright, Designs and Patents Act 1988

A CIP record for this book
is available from the British Library

ISBN 987–0–571–23096–9 (cased)
0–571–23096–2

987–0–571–23098–3 (limited edition)
0–571–23098–9

2 4 6 8 10 9 7 5 3 1

for Ann Saddlemyer

Call her Augusta
Because we arrived in August, and from now on
This month's baled hay and blackberries and combines
Will spell Augusta's bounty.

Contents

Notes and Acknowledgements

These poems first appeared, some in slightly different versions, in
*Agenda, Agni, Harvard Review, Irish Pages, Metre, Poetry Ireland
Review, Poetry London, Pretext 11, Scintilla, Guardian, Irish
Examiner, Irish Times, London Review of Books, New York
Review of Books, Salmagundi, Tatler, The New Yorker, The Yellow
Nib, Times Literary Supplement, Village, Waxwing Poems.*

A number of the poems also appeared in *A Shiver* (Clutag, 2005).
'Anything Can Happen', along with a short essay and several
translations, was included in a publication with that same title
(Amnesty/Town House, 2004). 'Tall Dames' is adapted from 'A
Gate Left Open', a programme note for the Dublin performance of
Janáček's 'Diary of One Who Vanished' (Gaiety Theatre,
14–16 October, 1999). 'On the Spot' was commissioned by
Maurice Riordan and John Burnside for their anthology, *Wild
Reckoning* (Picador, 2004). 'Saw Music' appeared in *The Door
Stands Open* (Irish Writers' Centre, 2005).

'The soul exceeds its circumstances' (p. 56) is quoted from Leon
Wieseltier's appreciation of Czeslaw Milosz, *New York Times
Book Review*, 12 September 2004. The lines quoted in 'To George
Seferis in the Underworld' are from his poem, 'On Aspalathoi',
translated by Edmund Keeley and Philip Sherrard (*Complete
Poems*, Princeton University Press, 1995); the epigraph is
from Roderick Beaton's *George Seferis, Waiting for the Angel*
(Yale University Press, 2003).

DISTRICT AND CIRCLE

The Turnip-Snedder

for Hughie O'Donoghue

In an age of bare hands
and cast iron,

the clamp-on meat-mincer,
the double-flywheeled water-pump,

it dug its heels in among wooden tubs
and troughs of slops,

hotter than body heat
in summertime, cold in winter

as winter's body armour,
a barrel-chested breast-plate

standing guard
on four braced greaves.

'This is the way that God sees life,'
it said, 'from seedling-braird to snedder,'

as the handle turned
and turnip-heads were let fall and fed

to the juiced-up inner blades,
'This is the turnip-cycle,'

as it dropped its raw sliced mess,
bucketful by glistering bucketful.

A Shiver

The way you had to stand to swing the sledge,
Your two knees locked, your lower back shock-fast
As shields in a *testudo*, spine and waist
A pivot for the tight-braced, tilting rib-cage;
The way its iron head planted the sledge
Unyieldingly as a club-footed last;
The way you had to heft and then half-rest
Its gathered force like a long-nursed rage
About to be let fly: does it do you good
To have known it in your bones, directable,
Withholdable at will,
A first blow that could make air of a wall,
A last one so unanswerably landed
The staked earth quailed and shivered in the handle?

Polish Sleepers

Once they'd been block-built criss-cross and
    four-squared
We lived with them and breathed pure creosote
Until they were laid and landscaped in a kerb,
A moulded verge, half-skirting, half-stockade,
Soon fringed with hardy ground-cover and grass.
But as that bulwark bleached in sun and rain
And the washed gravel pathway showed no stain,
Under its parched riverbed
Flinch and crunch I imagined tarry pus
Accruing, bearing forward to the garden
Wafts of what conspired when I'd lie
Listening for the goods from Castledawson . . .
Each languid, clanking waggon,
And afterwards, *rust, thistles, silence, sky.*

Anahorish 1944

'We were killing pigs when the Americans arrived.
A Tuesday morning, sunlight and gutter-blood
Outside the slaughterhouse. From the main road
They would have heard the squealing,
Then heard it stop and had a view of us
In our gloves and aprons coming down the hill.
Two lines of them, guns on their shoulders, marching.
Armoured cars and tanks and open jeeps.
Sunburnt hands and arms. Unknown, unnamed,
Hosting for Normandy.
            Not that we knew then
Where they were headed, standing there like
    youngsters
As they tossed us gum and tubes of coloured sweets.'

To Mick Joyce in Heaven

1

Kit-bag to tool-bag,
Warshirt to workshirt –
Out of your element
Among farmer in-laws,
The way you tied sheaves
The talk of the country,
But out on your own
When skylined on scaffolds –
A demobbed Achilles
Who was never a killer,
The strongest instead
Of the world's stretcher-bearers,
Turning your hand
To the bricklaying trade.

2

Prince of the sandpiles,
Hod-hoplite commander
Watching the wall,
Plumbing and pointing
From pegged-out foundation
To first course to cornice,
Keeping an eye
On the eye in the level
Before the cement set:
Medical orderly,

Bedpanner, bandager
Transferred to the home front,
Rising and shining
In brass-buttoned drab.

3

You spoke of 'the forces'.
Had served in the desert,
Been strafed and been saved
By courses of blankets
Fresh-folded and piled
Like bales on a field.
No sandbags that time.
A softness preserved you.
You spoke of sex also,
Talked man to man,
Took me for granted:
The English, you said,
Would do it on Sundays
Upstairs, in the daytime.

4

The weight of the trowel,
That's what surprised me.
You'd lift its lozenge-shaped
Blade in the air
To sever a brick
In a flash, and then twirl it
Fondly and lightly.
But whenever you sent me
To wash it and dry it

And you had your smoke,
Its iron was heavy,
Its sloped-angle handle
So thick-spanned and daunting
I needed two hands.

5

'To Mick Joyce in Heaven' –
The title just came to me,
Mick, and I started
If not quite from nowhere,
Then somewhere far off:
A bedroom, bright morning,
A man and a woman,
Their backs to the bedhead
And me at the foot.
It was your first leave,
A stranger arrived
In a house with no upstairs,
But heaven enough
To be going on with.

The Aerodrome

First it went back to grass, then after that
To warehouses and brickfields (designated
The Creagh Meadows Industrial Estate),
Its wartime grey control tower rebuilt and glazed

Into a hard-edged CEO-style villa:
Toome Aerodrome had turned to local history.
Hangars, runways, bomb stores, Nissen huts,
The perimeter barbed wire, forgotten and gone.

But not a smell of daisies and hot tar
On a newly-surfaced cart-road, Easter Monday,
1944. And not, two miles away that afternoon,
The annual bright booths of the fair at Toome,

All the brighter for having been denied.
No catchpenny stalls for us, no
Awnings, bonnets, or beribboned gauds:
Wherever the world was, we were somewhere else,

Had been and would be. Sparrows might fall,
B-26 Marauders not return, but the sky above
That land usurped by a compulsory order
Watched and waited – like me and her that day

Watching and waiting by the perimeter.
A fear crossed over then like the fly-by-night
And sun-repellent wing that flies by day
Invisibly above: would she rise and go

With the pilot calling from his Thunderbolt?
But for her part, in response, only the slightest
Back-stiffening and standing of her ground
As her hand reached down and tightened around
   mine.

If self is a location, so is love:
Bearings taken, markings, cardinal points,
Options, obstinacies, dug heels and distance,
Here and there and now and then, a stance.

Anything Can Happen

after Horace, *Odes*, 1, 34

Anything can happen. You know how Jupiter
Will mostly wait for clouds to gather head
Before he hurls the lightning? Well, just now
He galloped his thunder cart and his horses

Across a clear blue sky. It shook the earth
And the clogged underearth, the River Styx,
The winding streams, the Atlantic shore itself.
Anything can happen, the tallest towers

Be overturned, those in high places daunted,
Those overlooked regarded. Stropped-beak Fortune
Swoops, making the air gasp, tearing the crest off one,
Setting it down bleeding on the next.

Ground gives. The heaven's weight
Lifts up off Atlas like a kettle-lid.
Capstones shift, nothing resettles right.
Telluric ash and fire-spores boil away.

Helmet

Bobby Breen's. His Boston fireman's gift
With BREEN in scarlet letters on its spread
Fantailing brim,

Tinctures of sweat and hair oil
In the withered sponge and shock-absorbing webs
Beneath the crown –

Or better say the crest, for crest it is –
Leather-trimmed, steel-ridged, hand-tooled,
    hand-sewn,
Tipped with a little bud of beaten copper . . .

Bobby Breen's badged helmet's on my shelf
These twenty years, 'the headgear
Of the tribe', as O'Grady called it

In right heroic mood that afternoon
When the fireman-poet presented it to me
As 'the visiting fireman' –

As if I were up to it, as if I had
Served time under it, his fire-thane's shield,
His shoulder-awning, while shattering glass

And rubble-bolts out of a burning roof
Hailed down on every hatchet man and hose man
    there
Till the hard-reared shield-wall broke.

Out of Shot

November morning sunshine on my back
This bell-clear Sunday, elbows lodged strut-firm
On the unseasonably warm
Top bar of a gate, inspecting livestock,
Catching gleams of the distant Viking *vik*
Of Wicklow Bay; thinking *scriptorium*,
Norse raids, night-dreads and that 'fierce raiders'
    poem
About storm on the Irish Sea – so no attack
In the small hours or next morning; thinking shock
Out of the blue or blackout, the staggered walk
Of a donkey on the TV news last night –
Loosed from a cart that had loosed five mortar shells
In the bazaar district, wandering out of shot
Lost to its owner, lost for its sunlit hills.

Rilke: *After the Fire*

Early autumn morning hesitated,
Shying at newness, an emptiness behind
Scorched linden trees still crowding in around
The moorland house, now just one more wallstead

Where youngsters gathered up from god knows where
Hunted and yelled and ran wild in a pack.
Yet all of them fell silent when he appeared,
The son of the place, and with a long forked stick

Dragged an out-of-shape old can or kettle
From under hot, half burnt-away house-beams;
And then, like one with a doubtful tale to tell,
Turned to the others present, at great pains

To make them realize what had stood so.
For now that it was gone, it all seemed
Far stranger: more fantastical than Pharaoh.
And he was changed: a foreigner among them.

District and Circle

Tunes from a tin whistle underground
Curled up a corridor I'd be walking down
To where I knew I was always going to find
My watcher on the tiles, cap by his side,
His fingers perked, his two eyes eyeing me
In an unaccusing look I'd not avoid,
Or not just yet, since both were out to see
For ourselves.
            As the music larked and capered
I'd trigger and untrigger a hot coin
Held at the ready, but now my gaze was lowered
For was our traffic not in recognition?
Accorded passage, I would re-pocket and nod,
And he, still eyeing me, would also nod.

~

Posted, eyes front, along the dreamy ramparts
Of escalators ascending and descending
To a monotonous slight rocking in the works,
We were moved along, upstanding.
Elsewhere, underneath, an engine powered,
Rumbled, quickened, evened, quieted.
The white tiles gleamed. In passages that flowed
With draughts from cooler tunnels, I missed the
    light
Of all-overing, long since mysterious day,
Parks at lunchtime where the sunners lay
On body-heated mown grass regardless,
A resurrection scene minutes before

The resurrection, habitués
Of their garden of delights, of staggered summer.

~

Another level down, the platform thronged.
I re-entered the safety of numbers,
A crowd half straggle-ravelled and half strung
Like a human chain, the pushy newcomers
Jostling and purling underneath the vault,
On their marks to be first through the doors,
Street-loud, then succumbing to herd-quiet . . .
Had I betrayed or not, myself or him?
Always new to me, always familiar,
This unrepentant, now repentant turn
As I stood waiting, glad of a first tremor,
Then caught up in the now-or-never whelm
Of one and all the full length of the train.

~

Stepping on to it across the gap,
On to the carriage metal, I reached to grab
The stubby black roof-wort and take my stand
From planted ball of heel to heel of hand
As sweet traction and heavy down-slump stayed me.
I was on my way, well girded, yet on edge,
Spot-rooted, buoyed, aloof,
Listening to the dwindling noises off,
My back to the unclosed door, the platform empty;
And wished it could have lasted,
That long between-times pause before the budge
And glaze-over, when any forwardness
Was unwelcome and bodies readjusted,
Blindsided to themselves and other bodies.

~

So deeper into it, crowd-swept, strap-hanging,
My lofted arm a-swivel like a flail,
My father's glazed face in my own waning
And craning . . .
                              Again the growl
Of shutting doors, the jolt and one-off treble
Of iron on iron, then a long centrifugal
Haulage of speed through every dragging socket.

And so by night and day to be transported
Through galleried earth with them, the only relict
Of all that I belonged to, hurtled forward,
Reflecting in a window mirror-backed
By blasted weeping rock-walls.
                              Flicker-lit.

To George Seferis in the Underworld

The men began arguing about the spiky bushes that were in
brilliant yellow bloom on the slopes: were they caltrop or gorse?
... 'That reminds me of something,' said George.
'I don't know . . .'

That greeny stuff about your feet
is asphodel and rightly so,
but why do I think *seggans*?

And of a spring day
in your days of '71: Poseidon
making waves in sea and air
around Cape Sounion, its very name
all ozone-breeze and cavern-boom,
too utterly this-worldly, George, for you
intent upon an otherworldly scene
somewhere just beyond
the summit ridge, the cutting edge
of not remembering.

The bloody light. To hell with it.
Close eyes and concentrate.
Not crown of thorns, not sceptre reed
or Herod's court, but ha!
you had it! A harrowing, yes, in hell:
the hackle-spikes
that Plato told of, the tyrant's fate
in a passage you would quote:
'They bound him hand and foot,
they flung him down and flayed him,

gashing his flesh on thorny *aspalathoi*
and threw him into Tartarus, torn to shreds.'

As was only right
for a tyrant. But still, for you, maybe
too much i' the right, too black and white,
if still your chance to strike
against his ilk,
a last word meant to break
your much contested silence.

And for me a chance to test the edge
of *seggans*, dialect blade
hoar and harder and more hand-to-hand
than what is common usage nowadays:
sedge – marshmallow, rubber-dagger stuff.

Wordsworth's Skates

Star in the window.
                      Slate scrape.
                                        Bird or branch?
Or the whet and scud of steel on placid ice?

Not the bootless runners lying toppled
In dust in a display case,
Their bindings perished,

But the reel of them on frozen Windermere
As he flashed from the clutch of earth along its curve
And left it scored.

The Harrow-Pin

We'd be told, 'If you don't behave
There'll be nothing in your Christmas stocking for you
But an old kale stalk.' And we would believe him.

But if kale meant admonition, a harrow pin
Was correction's veriest unit.
Head-banged spike, forged fang, a true dead ringer

Out of a harder time, it was a stake
He'd drive through aspiration and pretence
For our instruction.

Let there once be any talk of decoration,
A shelf for knick-knacks, a picture-hook or -rail,
And the retort was instant: 'Drive a harrow-pin.'

Brute-forced, rusted, haphazardly set pins
From harrows wrecked by horse-power over stones
Lodged in the stable wall and on them hung

Horses' collars lined with sweat-veined ticking,
Old cobwebbed reins and hames and eye-patched
    winkers,
The tackle of the mighty, simple dead.

Out there, in musts of bedding cut with piss
He put all to the test. Inside, in the house,
Ungulled, irreconcilable

And horse-sensed as the travelled Gulliver,
What virtue he approved (and would assay)
Was in hammered iron.

Poet to Blacksmith

Eoghan Rua Ó Súilleabháin's (1748–84) instructions to
Séamus MacGearailt, translated from the Irish

Séamus, make me a side-arm to take on the earth,
A suitable tool for digging and grubbing the ground,
Lightsome and pleasant to lean on or cut with or lift,
Tastily finished and trim and right for the hand.

No trace of the hammer to show on the sheen of the blade,
The thing to have purchase and spring and be fit for the
    strain,
The shaft to be socketed in dead true and dead straight,
And I'll work with the gang till I drop and never complain.

The plate and the edge of it not to be wrinkly or crooked –
I see it well shaped from the anvil and sharp from the file;
The grain of the wood and the line of the shaft nicely
    fitted,
And best thing of all, the ring of it, sweet as a bell.

Midnight Anvil

If I wasn't there
When Barney Devlin hammered
The midnight anvil
I can still hear it: twelve blows
Struck for the millennium.

~

His nephew heard it
In Edmonton, Alberta:
The cellular phone
Held high as a horse's ear,
Barney smiling to himself.

~

Afterwards I thought
Church bels beyond the starres heard
And then imagined
Barney putting it to me:
'You'll maybe write a poem.'

~

What I'll do instead
Is quote those waterburning
Medieval smiths:
'Huf, puf! Lus, bus! Col!' *Such noise*
On nights heard no one never.

~

And Eoghan Rua
Asking Séamus MacGearailt
To forge him a spade
Sharp, well shaped from the anvil,
And ringing *sweet as a bell.*

Súgán

The fluster of that soft supply and feed –
Hay being coaxed in handfuls from a ruck,
Paid out to be taken in by furl and swivel,
Turned and tightened, rickety-rick, to rope –

Though just as often at the other end
I'd manipulate the hook,
Walking backwards, winding for all I was worth
By snag and by sag the long and the short of it
To make ends mesh –
                    in my left hand
The cored and threaded elderberry haft,
In my right the fashioned wire,
                              breeze on my back,
Sun in my face, a power to bind and loose
Eked out and into each last tug and lap.

Senior Infants

1 The Sally Rod

On the main street of Granard I met Duffy
Whom I had known before the age of reason
In short trousers in the Senior Infants' room
Where once upon a winter's day Miss Walls
Lost her head and cut the legs off us
For dirty talk we didn't think she'd hear.
'Well, for Jesus' sake,' cried Duffy, coming at me
With his stick in the air and two wide open arms,
'For Jesus' sake! D'you mind the sally rod?'

2 A Chow

I'm staring at the freshly scratched initials
Of Robert Donnelly in the sandstone coping
Of Anahorish Bridge, with Robert Donnelly
Beside me, also staring at them.
                                     'Here,' he says,
'Have a chow of this stuff,' stripping a dulse-thin film
Off the unwrapped ounce of Warhorse Plug –
Bog-bank brown, embossed, forbidden man-fruit
He's just been sent to buy for his father, Jock.

The roof of my mouth is thatch set fire to
At the burning-out of a neighbour, I want to lick
Bran from a bucket, grit off the coping stone.
'You have to spit,' says Robert, 'a chow's no good
Unless you spit like hell,' his ginger calf's lick
Like a scorch of flame, his quid-spurt fulgent.

3 One Christmas Day in the Morning

Tommy Evans must be sixty now as well. The last time I saw him was at the height of the Troubles, in Phil McKeever's pub in Castledawson, the first time we'd met since Anahorish School. I felt as free as a bird, a Catholic at large in Tommy's airspace.

Yet something small prevailed. My father balked at a word like 'Catholic' being used in company. Phil asked if we were OK. Tommy's crowd fenced him with 'What are you having, Tommy?'

I was blabbing on about guns, how they weren't a Catholic thing, how the sight of the one in his house had always scared me, how our very toys at Christmas proved my point – when his eye upon me narrowed.

I remembered his air-gun broken over his forearm, my envy of the polished hardwood stock, him thumbing the pellets into their aperture. The snick of the thing then as he clipped it shut and danced with his eye on the sights through a quick-quick angle of ninety degrees and back, then drilled the pair of us left-right to the back of the house.

The Evans' chicken coop was the shape of a sentry-box, walls and gable of weathered tongue-and-groove, the roofing-felt plied tight and tacked to the eaves. And there above the neat-hinged door, balanced on the very tip of the apex, was Tommy's target: the chrome lid of the bell of his father's bike. Whose little zings fairly brought me to my senses.

The Nod

Saturday evenings we would stand in line
In Loudan's butcher shop. Red beef, white string,
Brown paper ripped straight off for parcelling
Along the counter edge. Rib roast and shin
Plonked down, wrapped up, and bow-tied neat and
    clean
But seeping blood. Like dead weight in a sling,
Heavier far than I had been expecting
While my father shelled out for it, coin by coin.

Saturday evenings too the local B-Men,
Unbuttoned but on duty, thronged the town,
Neighbours with guns, parading up and down,
Some nodding at my father almost past him
As if deliberately they'd aimed and missed him
Or couldn't seem to place him, not just then.

A Clip

Harry Boyle's one-room, one-chimney house
With its settle bed was our first barber shop.
We'd go not for a haircut but 'a clip':
Cold smooth creeping steel and snicking scissors,
The strong-armed chair, the plain mysteriousness
Of your sheeted self inside that neck-tied cope –
Half sleeveless surplice, half hoodless Ku Klux cape.
Harry Boyle's one-roomed, old bog-road house
Near enough to home but unfamiliar:
What was it happened there?
Weeds shoulder-high up to the open door,
Harry not shaved, close breathing in your ear,
Loose hair in windfalls blown across the floor
Under the collie's nose. The collie's stare.

Edward Thomas on the Lagans Road

He's not in view but I can hear a step
On the grass-crowned road, the whip of daisy heads
On the toes of boots.
                              Behind the hedge
Eamon Murphy and Teresa Brennan –
Fully clothed, strong-arming each other –
Have sensed him and gone quiet. I keep on watching
As they rise and go.
                              And now the road is empty.
Nothing but air and light between their love-nest
And the bracken hillside where I lie alone.

Utter evening, as it was in the beginning,

Until the remembered come and go of lovers
Brings on his long-legged self on the Lagans Road –
Edward Thomas in his khaki tunic
Like one of the Evans brothers out of Leitrim,
Demobbed, 'not much changed', sandy moustached
    and freckled
From being, they said, with Monty in the desert.

Found Prose

1 The Lagans Road

The Lagans Road ran for about three quarters of a mile across an area of wetlands. It was one of those narrow country roads with weeds in the middle, grass verges and high hedges on either side, and all around it marsh and rushes and little shrubs and birch trees. For a minute or two every day, therefore, you were in the wilderness, but on the first morning I went to school it was as if the queen of elfland was leading me away. The McNicholls were neighbours and Philomena McNicholl had been put in charge of me during those first days. Ginger hair, freckled face, green gymfrock – a fey, if ever there was one. I remember my first sight of the school, a couple of low-set Nissen huts raising their corrugated backs above the hedges. From about a quarter of a mile away I could see youngsters running about in the road in front of the buildings and hear shouting in the playground. Years later, when I read an account of how the Indians of the Pacific Northwest foresaw their arrival in the land of the dead – coming along a forest path where other travellers' cast-offs lay scattered on the bushes, hearing voices laughing and calling, knowing there was a life in the clearing up ahead that would be familiar, but feeling at the same time lost and homesick – it struck me I had already experienced that kind of arrival. Next thing in the porch I was faced with rows of coathooks nailed up at different heights along the wall, so that everyone in the different classes could reach them, everyone had a place to hang overcoat or scarf and proceed to the strange room, where our names were new in the rollbook and would soon be called.

2 Tall Dames

Even though we called them 'the gypsies', we knew that gypsies were properly another race. They inhabited the land of eros, glimpsed occasionally when the circus rolled into a field and a fortune-teller, swathed in her silks and beads, inclined to us from the back door of a caravan. The people we called 'the gypsies' we would now call travellers, although at that time in that place 'tinker' was an honourable term, signifying tin-smiths, white-smiths, pony-keepers, regulars on the doorstep, squatters on the long acre. Marvellous upfront women in unerotic woollen shawls, woven in big tartan patterns of tan and mossy green, their baskets full of dyed wooden flowers, their speech cadenced to beg and keep begging with all the stamina of a cantor. Walking the roads in ones and twos, children on their arms or at their heels. Squaws of the ditchback, in step with Yeats's 'tall dames' walking in Avalon.

You encountered them in broad daylight, going about their usual business, yet there was always a feeling that they were coming towards you out of storytime. One of the menfolk on the road with a bit of a halter, you on your way to school, he with a smell of woodsmoke off him, asking if you'd seen an old horse anywhere behind the hedges. The stillness of the low tarpaulin tent as you approached and passed, the green wood in the fire spitting under a pot slung from a tripod. Every time they landed in the district, there was an extra-ness in the air, as if a gate had been left open in the usual life, as if something might get in or get out.

3 Boarders

There's no heat in the bus, but the engine's running and up where a destination should be showing it just says PRIVATE, so it must be ours. We're back in the days of peaked caps and braid piping, drivers mounting steps as ominously as hangmen, conductors with plump bags of coin, the ticket punch a-dangle on its chain. But this is a special bus, so there'll be no tickets, no conductor and no fare collection until the load is full.

The stops are the same as every other time, clusters of us with suitcases assembled in shop doorways or at the appointed crossroads, the old bus getting up speed wherever the going's good, but now she's changing down on Glenshane Pass. The higher she goes, the heavier she pulls, and yet there's no real hurry. Let the driver keep doing battle with the gear-stick, let his revs and double-clutchings drag the heart, anything to put off that last stop when he slows down at the summit and turns and seems about to take us back. Instead of which he halts, pulls on the handbrake, gives us time to settle, then switches off.

When we start again, the full lock of the steering will be held, the labour of cut and spin leave tyre-marks in the gravel, the known country fall away behind us. But for the moment it's altogether quiet, the whole bus shakes as he bangs the cabin door shut, comes round the side and in to lift the money. Unfamiliar, uninvolved, almost, it seems, angered, he deals with us one by one, as one by one we go farther into ourselves, wishing we were him on the journey back, flailing downhill with the windows all lit up, empty and faster and angrier bend after bend.

The Lift

A first green braird: the hawthorn half in leaf.
Her funeral filled the road
And could have stepped from some old photograph

Of a Breton *pardon*, remote
Familiar women and men in caps
Walking four abreast, soon falling quiet.

Then came the throttle and articulated whops
Of a helicopter crossing, and afterwards
Awareness of the sound of our own footsteps,

Of open air, and the life behind those words
'Open' and 'air'. I remembered her aghast,
Foetal, shaking, sweating, shrunk, wet-haired,

A beaten breath, a misting mask, the flash
Of one wild glance, like ghost surveillance
From behind a gleam of helicopter glass.

A lifetime, then the deathtime: reticence
Keeping us together when together,
All declaration deemed outspokeness.

Favourite aunt, good sister, faithful daughter,
Delicate since childhood, tough alloy
Of disapproval, kindness and *hauteur*,

She took the risk, at last, of certain joys –
Her birdtable and jubilating birds,
The 'fashion' in her wardrobe and her tallboy.

Weather, in the end, would say our say.
Reprise of griefs in summer's clearest mornings,
Children's deaths in snowdrops and the may,

Whole requiems at the sight of plants and gardens . . .
They bore her lightly on the bier. Four women,
Four friends – she would have called them girls –
    stepped in

And claimed the final lift beneath the hawthorn.

Nonce Words

The road taken
to bypass Cavan
took me west,
(a sign mistaken)
so at Derrylin
I turned east.

Sun on ice,
white floss
on reed and bush,
the bridge-iron cast
in an Advent silence
I drove across,

then pulled in,
parked, and sat
breathing mist
on the windscreen.
Requiescat . . .
I got out

well happed up,
stood at the frozen
shore gazing
at rimed horizon,
my first stop
like this in years.

And blessed myself
in the name of the nonce
and happenstance,
the *Who knows*
and *What nexts*
and *So be its.*

Stern

in memory of Ted Hughes

'And what was it like,' I asked him,
'Meeting Eliot?'
                'When he looked at you,'
He said, 'it was like standing on a quay
Watching the prow of the *Queen Mary*
Come towards you, very slowly.'

         Now it seems
I'm standing on a pierhead watching him
All the while watching me as he rows out
And a wooden end-stopped stern
Labours and shimmers and dips,
Making no real headway.

Out of This World

in memory of Czeslaw Milosz

1 'Like everybody else . . .'

'Like everybody else, I bowed my head
during the consecration of the bread and wine,
lifted my eyes to the raised host and raised chalice,
believed (whatever it means) that a change occurred.

I went to the altar rails and received the mystery
on my tongue, returned to my place, shut my eyes fast,
    made
an act of thanksgiving, opened my eyes and felt
time starting up again.
                        There was never a scene
when I had it out with myself or with another.
The loss occurred off-stage. And yet I cannot
disavow words like "thanksgiving" or "host"
or "communion bread". They have an undying
tremor and draw, like well water far down.'

2 *Brancardier*

You're off, a pilgrim, in the age of steam:
Derry, Dun Laoghaire, Dover, Rue du Bac
(Prayers for the Blessed M. M. Alacoque,
That she be canonized). Then leisure time

That evening in Paris, whence to Lourdes,
Learning to trust your learning on the way:
'*Non, pas de vin, merci. Mais oui, du thé,*'
And the waiter's gone to take you at your word.

Hotel de quoi in *Rue de quoi*? All gone.
But not your designation, *brancardier*,
And your coloured bandolier, as you lift and lay
The sick on stretchers in precincts of the shrine

Or on bleak concrete to await their bath.
And always the word 'cure' hangs in the air
Like crutches hung up near the grotto altar.
And always prayers out loud or under breath.

Belgian miners in blue dungarees
March in procession, carrying brass lamps.
Sodalities with sashes, poles and pennants
Move up the line. Mantillas, rosaries

And the *unam sanctam catholicam* acoustic
Of that underground basilica – maybe
Not gone but not what was meant to be,
The concrete reinforcement of the Mystic-

al Body, the Eleusis of its age.
I brought back one plastic canteen litre
On a shoulder-strap (*très chic*) of the Lourdes water.
One small glass dome that englobed an image

Of the Virgin above barefoot Bernadette –
Shake it and the clear liquid would snow
Flakes like white angel feathers on the grotto.
And (for stretcher-bearing work) a certificate.

3 Saw Music

Q. Do you renounce the world?
A. I do renounce it.

Barrie Cooke has begun to paint 'godbeams',
Vents of brightness that make the light of heaven
Look like stretched sheets of fluted silk or rayon
In an old-style draper's window. Airslides, scrims

And scumble. Columnar sift. But his actual palette
Is ever sludge and smudge, as if a shower
Made puddles on the spirit's winnowing floor.
What it reminds me of is a wet night

In Belfast, around Christmas, when the man
Who played the saw inside the puddled doorway
Of a downtown shop, in light from a display
Of tinselled stuffs and sleigh bells blinking neon,

Started to draw his bow across the blade.
The stainless steel was oiled or Vaselined,
The saw stood upside down and his left hand
Pressed light or heavy as the tune required

Flop-wobble grace note or high banshee whine.
Rain spat upon his threadbare gaberdine,
Into his cap where the occasional tossed coin
Basked on damp lining, the raindrops glittering

[50]

Like the saw's greased teeth his bow caressed and
    crossed
Back across unharmed. 'The art of oil painting –
Daubs fixed on canvas – is a paltry thing
Compared with what cries out to be expressed,'

The poet said, who lies this god-beamed day
Coffined in Krakow, as out of this world now
As the untranscendent music of the saw
He might have heard in Vilnius or Warsaw

And would not have renounced, however paltry.

In Iowa

In Iowa once, among the Mennonites
In a slathering blizzard, conveyed all afternoon
Through sleet-glit pelting hard against the windscreen
And a wiper's strong absolving slumps and flits,

I saw, abandoned in the open gap
Of a field where wilted corn stalks flagged the snow,
A mowing machine. Snow brimmed its iron seat,
Heaped each spoked wheel with a thick white brow

And took the shine off oil in the black-toothed gears.
Verily I came forth from that wilderness
As one unbaptized who had known darkness
At the third hour and the veil in tatters.

In Iowa once. In the slush and rush and hiss
Not of parted but as of rising waters.

Höfn

The three-tongued glacier has begun to melt.
What will we do, they ask, when boulder-milt
Comes wallowing across the delta flats

And the miles-deep shag-ice makes its move?
I saw it, ridged and rock-set, from above,
Undead grey-gristed earth-pelt, aeon-scruff,

And feared its coldness that still seemed enough
To iceblock the plane window dimmed with breath,
Deepfreeze the seep of adamantine tilth

And every warm, mouthwatering word of mouth.

On the Spot

A cold clutch, a whole nestful, all but hidden
In last year's autumn leaf-mould, and I knew
By the mattness and the stillness of them, rotten,
Making death sweat of a morning dew
That didn't so much shine the shells as damp them.
I was down on my hands and knees there in the
     wet
Grass under the hedge, adoring it,
Early riser busy reaching in
And used to finding warm eggs. But instead
This sudden polar stud
And stigma and dawn stone-circle chill
In my mortified right hand, proof positive
Of what conspired on the spot to addle
Matter in its planetary stand-off.

The Tollund Man in Springtime

Into your virtual city I'll have passed
Unregistered by scans, screens, hidden eyes,
Lapping myself in time, an absorbed face
Coming and going, neither god nor ghost,
Not at odds or at one, but simply lost
To you and yours, out under seeding grass
And trickles of kesh water, sphagnum moss,
Dead bracken on the spreadfield, red as rust.
I reawoke to revel in the spirit
They strengthened when they chose to put me down
For their own good. And to a sixth-sensed threat:
Panicked snipe offshooting into twilight,
Then going awry, larks quietened in the sun,
Clear alteration in the bog-pooled rain.

~

Scone of peat, composite bog-dough
They trampled like a muddy vintage, then
Slabbed and spread and turned to dry in sun –
Though never kindling-dry the whole way through –
A dead-weight, slow-burn lukewarmth in the flue,
Ashless, flameless, its very smoke a sullen
Waft of swamp-breath . . . And me, so long unrisen,
I knew that same dead weight in joint and sinew
Until a spade-plate slid and soughed and plied
At my buried ear, and the levered sod
Got lifted up; then once I felt the air
I was like turned turf in the breath of God,
Bog-bodied on the sixth day, brown and bare,
And on the last, all told, unatrophied.

~

My heavy head. Bronze-buffed. Ear to the ground.
My eye at turf level. Its snailskin lid.
My cushioned cheek and brow. My phantom hand
And arm and leg and shoulder that felt pillowed
As fleshily as when the bog pith weighed
To mould me to itself and it to me
Between when I was buried and unburied.
Between what happened and was meant to be.
On show for years while all that lay in wait
Still waited. Disembodied. Far renowned.
Faith placed in me, me faithless as a stone
The harrow turned up when the crop was sown.
Out in the Danish night I'd hear soft wind
And remember moony water in a rut.

~

'The soul exceeds its circumstances.' Yes.
History not to be granted the last word
Or the first claim . . . In the end I gathered
From the display-case peat my staying powers,
Told my webbed wrists to be like silver birches,
My old uncallused hands to be young sward,
The spade-cut skin to heal, and got restored
By telling myself this. Late as it was,
The early bird still sang, the meadow hay
Still buttercupped and daisied, sky was new.
I smelled the air, exhaust fumes, silage reek,
Heard from my heather bed the thickened traffic
Swarm at a roundabout five fields away
And transatlantic flights stacked in the blue.

~

Cattle out in rain, their knowledgeable
Solid standing and readiness to wait,
These I learned from. My study was the wet,
My head as washy as a head of kale,
Shedding water like the flanks and tail
Of every dumb beast sunk above the cloot
In trampled gaps, bringing their heavyweight
Silence to bear on nosed-at sludge and puddle.
Of another world, unlearnable, and so
To be lived by, whatever it was I knew
Came back to me. Newfound contrariness.
In check-out lines, at cash-points, in those queues
Of wired, far-faced smilers, I stood off,
Bulrush, head in air, far from its lough.

~

Through every check and scan I carried with me
A bunch of Tollund rushes – roots and all –
Bagged in their own bog-damp. In an old stairwell
Broom cupboard where I had hoped they'd stay
Damp until transplanted, they went musty.
Every green-skinned stalk turned friable,
The drowned-mouse fibres withered and the whole
Limp, soggy cluster lost its frank bouquet
Of weed leaf and turf mould. Dust in my palm
And in my nostrils dust, should I shake it off
Or mix it in with spit in pollen's name
And my own? As a man would, cutting turf,
I straightened, spat on my hands, felt benefit
And spirited myself into the street.

Moyulla

In those days she flowed
black-lick and quick
under the sallies,
the coldness off her

like the coldness off you –
your cheek and your clothes
and your moves – when you come in
from gardening.

She was in the swim
of herself, her gravel shallows
swarmed, pollen sowings
tarnished her pools.

~

And so what, did I hear
somebody cry? Let them
cry if it suits them,
but let it be for her,

her stones, her purls, her pebbles
slicked and blurred
with algae, as if her name
and addressing water

suffered muddying,
her clear vowels

a great vowel shift,
Moyola to Moyulla.

~

Milk-fevered river.
Froth at the mouth
of the discharge pipe,
gidsome flotsam . . .

Barefooted on the bank,
glad-eyed, ankle-grassed,
I saw it all
and loved it at the time –

blettings, beestings,
creamery spillage
on her cleanly, comely
sally trees and alders.

~

Step into her for me
some fresh-faced afternoon,
but not before
you step into thigh waders

to walk up to the bib
upstream, in the give and take
of her deepest, draggiest purchase,
countering, parting,

getting back at her, sourcing
her and your plashy self,
neither of you
ready to let up.

Planting the Alder

For the bark, dulled argent, roundly wrapped
And pigeon-collared.

For the splitter-splatter, guttering
Rain-flirt leaves.

For the snub and clot of the first green cones,
Smelted emerald, chlorophyll.

For the scut and scat of cones in winter,
So rattle-skinned, so fossil-brittle.

For the alder-wood, flame-red when torn
Branch from branch.

But mostly for the swinging locks
Of yellow catkins,

Plant it, plant it,
Streel-head in the rain.

Tate's Avenue

Not the brown and fawn car rug, that first one
Spread on sand by the sea but breathing land-breaths,
Its vestal folds unfolded, its comfort zone
Edged with a fringe of sepia-coloured wool tails.

Not the one scraggy with crusts and eggshells
And olive stones and cheese and salami rinds
Laid out by the torrents of the Guadalquivir
Where we got drunk before the corrida.

Instead, again, it's locked-park Sunday Belfast,
A walled back yard, the dust-bins high and silent
As a page is turned, a finger twirls warm hair
And nothing gives on the rug or the ground beneath it.

I lay at my length and felt the lumpy earth,
Keen-sensed more than ever through discomfort,
But never shifted off the plaid square once.
When we moved I had your measure and you had mine.

A Hagging Match

Axe-thumps outside
like wave-hits through
a night ferry:
       you
whom I cleave to, hew to,
splitting firewood.

Fiddleheads

Fiddlehead ferns are a delicacy where? Japan? Estonia?
Ireland long ago?

I say Japan because when I think of those delicious
things I think of my friend Toraiwa, and the surprise I
felt when he asked me about the erotic. He said it
belonged in poetry and he wanted more of it.

So here they are, Toraiwa, frilled, infolded, tenderized,
in a little steaming basket, just for you.

To Pablo Neruda in Tamlaghtduff

Niall FitzDuff brought a jar
of crab-apple jelly
made from crabs off the tree
that grew at Duff's Corner –
still grows at Duff's Corner –
a tree I never once saw
with crab apples on it.

Contrary, unflowery
sky-whisk and bristle, more
twig-fret than fruit-fort,
crabbed
as crabbed could be –
that was the tree
I remembered.

But then –
O my Pablo of earthlife –
when I tasted the stuff
it was freshets and orbs.
My eyes were on stalks,
I was back in an old
rutted cart road, making
the rounds of the district, breasting
its foxgloves, smelling
cow-parsley and nettles, all
of high summer's smoulder
under our own tree ascendant
in Tamlaghtduff,

its crab-hoard and – yes,
in pure hindsight – corona
of gold.
      For now,
O my home-truth Neruda,
round-faced as the crowd
at the crossroads, with your eyes
I see it, now taste-bud
and tear-duct melt down
and I spread the jelly on thick
as if there were no tomorrow.

Home Help

1 Helping Sarah

And so with tuck and tightening of blouse
And vigorous advance of knee, she was young
Again as the year, out weeding rigs
In the same old skirt and brogues, on top of things
Every time she straightened. And a credit.

                      Her oatmeal tweed
With pinpoints of red haw and yellow whin,
Its threadbare workadayness hard and common;
Her quick step; her dry hand; all things well-sped;
Her open and closed relations with earth's work;
And everything passed on without a word.

2 Chairing Mary

Heavy, helpless, carefully manhandled
Upstairs every night in a wooden chair,
She sat in all day as the sun sundialled
Window-splays across the quiet floor . . .

Her body heat had entered the braced timber
Two would take hold of, by weighted leg and back,
Tilting and hoisting, the one on the lower step
Bearing the brunt, the one reversing up

Not averting eyes from her hurting bulk,
And not embarrassed, but never used to it.
I think of her warm brow we might have once
Bent to and kissed before we kissed it cold.

Rilke: *The Apple Orchard*

Come just after the sun has gone down, watch
This deepening of green in the evening sward:
Is it not as if we'd long since garnered
And stored within ourselves a something which

From feeling and from feeling recollected,
From new hope and half-forgotten joys
And from an inner dark infused with these,
Issues in thoughts as ripe as windfalls scattered

Here under trees like trees in a Dürer woodcut –
Pendent, pruned, the husbandry of years
Gravid in them until the fruit appears –
Ready to serve, replete with patience, rooted

In the knowledge that no matter how above
Measure or expectation, all must be
Harvested and yielded, when a long life willingly
Cleaves to what's willed and grows in mute
   resolve.

Quitting Time

The hosed-down chamfered concrete pleases him.
He'll wait a while before he kills the light
On the cleaned-up yard, its pails and farrowing crate,
And the cast-iron pump immobile as a herm
Upstanding elsewhere, in another time.
More and more this last look at the wet
Shine of the place is what means most to him –
And to repeat the phrase, 'My head is light',
Because it often is as he reaches back
And switches off, a home-based man at home
In the end with little. Except this same
Night after nightness, redding up the work,
The song of a tubular steel gate in the dark
As he pulls it to and starts his uphill trek.

Home Fires

1 A Scuttle for Dorothy Wordsworth

Dorothy young, jig-jigging her iron shovel,
Barracking a pile of lumpy coals
Carted up by one Thomas Ashburner,
Her toothache so ablaze the carter's name
Goes unremarked as every jolt and jag
Backstabs her through her wrist-bone, neck-bone,
    jaw-bone.

Dorothy old, doting at the flicker
In a brass companion set, all the companions
Gone or let go, their footfalls on the road
Unlistened for, that sounded once as plump
As the dropping shut of the flap-board scuttle-lid
The minute she'd stacked the grate for their
    arrival.

2 A Stove Lid for W. H. Auden

The mass and majesty of this world, all
    That carries weight and always weighs the same . . .
        'The Shield of Achilles'

The mass and majesty of this world I bring you
In the small compass of a cast-iron stove lid.
I was the youngster in a Fair Isle jersey
Who loved a lifter made of stainless steel,
The way its stub claw found its clink-fast hold,
The fit and weight and danger as it bore
The red hot solidus to one side of the stove
For the fire-fanged maw of the fire-box to be stoked,
Then the gnashing bucket stowed.
                    So one more time,
I tote it, hell-mouth stopper, flat-earth disc,
And replace it safely. Wherefore rake and rattle,
Watch sparks die in the ashpan, poke again,
Think of dark matter in the starlit coalhouse.

The Birch Grove

At the back of a garden, in earshot of river water,
In a corner walled off like the baths or bake-house
Of an unroofed abbey or broken-floored Roman villa,
They have planted their birch grove. Planted it recently
    only,
But already each morning it puts forth in the sun
Like their own long grown-up selves, the white of the
    bark
As suffused and cool as the white of the satin
    nightdress
She bends and straightens up in, pouring tea,
Sitting across from where he dandles a sandal
On his big time-keeping foot, as bare as an abbot's.
Red brick and slate, plum tree and apple retain
Their credibility, a CD of Bach is making the rounds
Of the common or garden air. Above them a jet trail
Tapers and waves like a willow wand or a taper.
'If art teaches us anything,' he says, trumping life
With a quote, 'it's that the human condition is private.'

Cavafy: 'The rest I'll speak of to the ones below in Hades'

'Yes,' said the proconsul, replacing the scroll,
'indeed the line is true. And beautiful.
Sophocles at his most philosophical.
We'll talk about a whole lot more down there
and be happy to be seen for what we are.
Here we're like sentries, watching anxiously,
guarding every locked-up hurt and secret,
but all we cover up here, day and night,
down there we'll let out, frankly and completely.'

'That is,' said the sophist, with a slow half-smile,
'if down there they ever talk about such things,
if they can be bothered with the like at all.'

In a Loaning

Spoken for in autumn, recovered speech
Having its way again, I gave a cry:
'Not beechen green, but these shin-deep coffers
Of copper-fired leaves, these beech boles grey.'

The Blackbird of Glanmore

On the grass when I arrive,
Filling the stillness with life,
But ready to scare off
At the very first wrong move.
In the ivy when I leave.

It's you, blackbird, I love.

I park, pause, take heed.
Breathe. Just breathe and sit
And lines I once translated
Come back: 'I want away
To the house of death, to my father

Under the low clay roof.'

And I think of one gone to him,
A little stillness dancer –
Haunter-son, lost brother –
Cavorting through the yard,
So glad to see me home,

My homesick first term over.

And think of a neighbour's words
Long after the accident:
'Yon bird on the shed roof,
Up on the ridge for weeks –
I said nothing at the time

But I never liked yon bird.'

The automatic lock
Clunks shut, the blackbird's panic
Is shortlived, for a second
I've a bird's eye view of myself,
A shadow on raked gravel

In front of my house of life.

Hedge-hop, I am absolute
For you, your ready talkback,
Your each stand-offish comeback,
Your picky, nervy goldbeak –
On the grass when I arrive,

In the ivy when I leave.